943   Schloredt,
SchL   Valerie.
West Germany, t...
land and its people

DATE DUE		PERMA-BOUND	
JAN 2 5			

Consultant Ute Uhde
Managing Editor Belinda Hollyer
Editor Beverley Birch
Project editor, U.S. edition Joanne Fink
Editor, U.S. edition Marie Norris
Design Danuta Trebus
Picture Research Kathy Lockley
Production Rosemary Bishop
Illustrations Paul Cooper
      Marilyn Day
      Ron Hayward
      Eric Jewel
      John Mousdale
      John Shackell
Maps Matthews & Taylor Associates
(pages 44–45)

Endpaper: Hillside vineyards and the village of Zell on the banks of the Mosel river.

Contents page: The market square in Trier.

Photographic sources Key to positions of illustrations (T) top, (C) center, (B) bottom, (L) left, (R) right.
Aldus Archive 16–17, 19(TL). Anthony Verlag 40(BL). Architectural Association 27(BR). Barnaby's Picture Library 18(TR). Nick Birch Cover(T&C), Endpapers, Contents page, 9(T), 11(BL), 27(TR), 29(TR), 29(BR), 32(TR), 33(TR), 33(B), 34(BL), 34–5, 35(TL), 35(BR), 36, 37(TR), 37(C), 39(B), 40–1(T), 41(TR). Bridgeman Art Library/Kunsthalle, Hamburg 23(BR). BBC Hulton Picture Library 15(BL), 19(BL). Camera Press 19(TR), 31(TR). J. Allan Cash 29(TL). Colorsport 41(BL). Courtauld Institute 13(TL), 22(TR). Mary Evans Picture Library 10(T), 10(B), 12, 13(R), 14(TR), 15(TR), 15(CR), 16(BL), 17(TL), 17(BR), 26(CR). Fotolink 21(BR). Gallerie Fisher-Lucerne 15(CL). Peter Haabjoern 11(TL), 38(C), 39(T). Interfoto 16(CR). Kobal Collection 23(TR). Photosource 18(BR). Popperfoto 23(CL), 25(R). Rex Features 20(B), 20–1(T), 30–1(T). Roger-Viollet 24(TR), 25(TL), 26(TR). Reg Wilson 24–5. Zefa Cover (B), 9(B), 28–9(B), 31(B), 38(BL).

First published in Great Britain in 1974 by Macdonald Educational Ltd.

This revised edition published in 1987 by Macdonald & Co (Publishers) Ltd London & Sydney
A BPCC plc company

Adapted and published in the United States in 1988 by Silver Burdett Press Inc., Prentice-Hall Building Englewood Cliffs, New Jersey

Library of Congress Cataloging-in-Publication Data

Schloredt, Valerie.
    West Germany, the land and its people/Valerie Schloredt. — Rev. ed.
       p.   cm. — (Silver Burdett countries)
    Includes index.
    Summary: Text and illustrations introduce the geography, history, people, and culture of West Germany.
    ISBN   ISBN
    0-382-09471-9   0-382-09478-6
(lib. bdg.) (pbk.)
    1. Germany (West) — Juvenile literature. [1. Germany (West)]   I. Title.   II. Series.
DD258.S35 1988
943—dc19   87-28468
                     CIP
                     AC

Silver Burdett
Countries

West
Germany

the land and its people

Valerie Schloredt

Silver Burdett Press
Englewood Cliffs, New Jersey

Contents

What is Germany?

Germany's changing borders

Germany has often been called the "land in the middle," describing its central position in Europe. With few natural geographic borders, it has been subject to the influences of many different cultures and nationalities.

Historically it has often been difficult to define Germany as a nation and to unify the country under one central government. For example, in the seventeenth century the area that is now West and East Germany was part of the "Holy Roman Empire of the German Nation." This consisted of 1800 separate towns and principalities extending as far as the territory of modern-day Poland, Czechoslovakia, Luxembourg, France, and Austria.

Germany was not unified as one nation until the "German Empire" of 1871; but this unity was to be short-lived. After the defeat of Germany in World War II, the country was divided into zones of occupation by the armies of the Allied nations. The Soviet zone was in the east; the British, French, and American zones in the west.

When there was disagreement between the nations over the organization and administration of post-war Germany, the Soviets began organizing the eastern zone according to their own socialist economic and political system. The British, French, and Americans organized their three zones according to Western democratic ideas.

East and West Germany

Two new German states, East Germany, correctly known as the German Democratic Republic or GDR, and West Germany, the Federal Republic of Germany, were both founded in 1949.

Though East and West Germany share a common language and history, they have developed along very different lines since they were formed. As time passes it seems doubtful that the two will ever be reunited as many Germans had hoped in the years following the war.

The 858-mile-long border between the GDR and the FRG was closed by the East German authorities in 1952 to halt the flow of people to the west. This closed border is fortified with fences, watch-towers, and mines and guarded by East German soldiers. In the Cold War years immediately following the war, when relations between the United States and the Soviet Union were especially strained, the East German border was what many people in the West thought of as the "Iron Curtain." This was a term coined by the British prime minister Winston Churchill to describe the political differences and barriers between the U.S. and its allies in western Europe on the one hand, and the Soviet Union and the socialist countries of eastern Europe on the other.

West Germany today

The Federal Republic of Germany, commonly called the FRG or West Germany, is today bordered by nine countries. It extends from the Baltic and North Sea coastlines to the border with Switzerland and Austria 500 miles to the south.

The natural contrasts of the landscape vary from flat northern plains to central uplands where picturesque river valleys cut through rolling hills. A tradition of regionalism goes back to the days when Germany was divided into independent kingdoms. Today the Federal Republic of Germany consists of West Berlin and ten states or *Länder* that approximate earlier regions of western Germany.

▲ The landscapes of West Germany vary from golden farmland to the skyscrapers of central Frankfurt (right).

◄ **The ten states of the Federal Republic**
Schleswig-Holstein is the northernmost state of the FRG. It shares a border with Denmark to the north and has the most coastline in West Germany, with the Baltic in the east and the North Sea to the west. The capital city is Kiel.

Just south of Schleswig-Holstein is the city-state of *Hamburg* on the river Elbe. Hamburg has been an important port since the time of the Hanseatic League in the thirteenth century.

The state of *Lower Saxony* is mainly flat, agricultural land. Its capital city is Hanover. Within the territory of Lower Saxony lies the city-state of *Bremen*, the smallest state in the FRG.

North Rhine-Westphalia is the most heavily industrialized of the ten states. Its capital city is Düsseldorf.

Hesse is a largely agricultural state. The capital city, Wiesbaden, is a popular health resort.

The *Rhineland-Palatinate* includes some of the most beautiful scenery along the Rhine. The capital is Mainz.

The coal-rich industrial region of the *Saar* was attached to France after World War II and was only returned to West Germany in 1957. Its capital is Saarbrücken.

Baden-Württemberg was created from three different states in 1951. Its capital is Stuttgart.

Bavaria with its alpine scenery and lively capital city of Munich is a favorite destination for tourists to West Germany.

West Berlin, located within the territory of East Germany, is still administered in part by the Occupying Powers. It is sometimes treated as the eleventh state of West Germany.

The German people

German tribes

Sometime during the second century B.C. Germanic tribes from southern Scandinavia and present-day Denmark began moving down into the plain that covers much of northern Europe including what is now northern Germany. The Germanic tribes were well established in Germany by the time the Roman Emperor Julius Caesar set out to conquer Gaul (present-day France) in 58 B.C.

When Roman legions marched north into Germany to conquer territory for Rome, they met with fierce resistance from the German tribes, and never succeeded in expanding the Roman Empire north of the Danube or east of the Rhine into central Germany.

Around the fourth century A.D. a mass migration of Germanic peoples began which affected all of Europe. Germanic tribes crossed into Roman territory. Rome was repeatedly invaded, and lost much of its former power.

The Holy Roman Empire

The Franks were a Germanic tribe who lived in what is now France and in southern and western Germany. They emerged as the most powerful of the Germanic tribes after the fall of Rome. They were ruled by their king, Clovis, who converted to Christianity in 496. His subjects followed his example, and Christianity was further spread through Germany by monks from Britain.

After Clovis the German tribes were joined together by the Frankish King Charlemagne (742–814) in a kingdom that covered present-day Germany, France, and northern Italy. The leaders of the Christian church in Rome promised to support Charlemagne's rule in exchange for military protection, and on Christmas Day in A.D. 800, the Pope crowned Charlemagne "Holy Roman Emperor." Charlemagne eventually made the town of Aachen the center of his empire, which he enlarged to spread all over Europe.

The Holy Roman Empire was later divided mainly into the Kingdom of the West Franks (later to become France), and the Kingdom of the East Franks, covering much of what is now Germany.

From the ninth to the thirteenth century, the emperors of the eastern kingdom were crowned by the Pope in Rome, though they reigned over only a fragment of the former Holy Roman Empire.

Conflicts between the emperors and Church authority in Rome led to a decline in the authority of Holy Roman Emperors, while the local power of feudal princes grew stronger all over Germany.

The German language

Modern German belongs to the same language group (Western Indo-European) as Dutch, English, Norwegian, and Swedish. These are all called "Germanic" languages, having common origins in the variety of different dialects spoken by the early Germanic tribes. There was no standard German language until about 1100, when monks in southern Germany began writing in what was later called "Middle High German."

Today, even though "High German" is the official language of West and East Germany, differences in dialect still persist. The "Low German" dialect of the early Middle Ages is still spoken in some areas in northern Germany, and regional differences in both accent and vocabulary are still common throughout all of Germany.

▲ As the first Holy Roman Emperor, Charlemagne helped to preserve Western civilization after the fall of Rome. He encouraged the founding of monasteries and the spread of education.

▼ A Roman commander with German followers. The tribes who lived within Roman territory were influenced by colonization and adopted Roman customs in the cities of Trier, Cologne, Augsburg, and Bonn.

10

◀ This village is a reconstruction of dwellings built by prehistoric Stone Age people in the village of Unteruhldingen on Lake Constance. Germany is rich in artifacts of early human habitation. Skeletal remains of Neanderthals who lived 50,000 years ago were discovered in a valley near Düsseldorf in 1856.

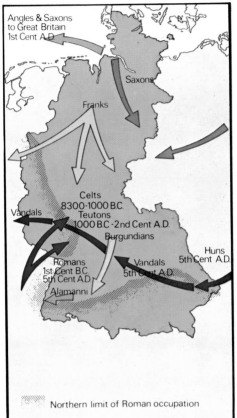

▲ Germany's position in the center of Europe made it a crossroads during periods of migration, when tribes set out in search of better land, to escape other invading tribes, or to conquer and plunder other lands. The movement was southward and westward: as the Angles and Saxons sailed to Britain, Burgundians moved toward France, and the Vandals went through Spain to northern Africa.

◀ The notion that Germans are all blonde-haired and blue-eyed is a myth. Like other Europeans they are a mixture of different physical types. The variety in appearance of modern Germans stems from the days of the Germanic migrations in the first to the fifth centuries A.D. as well as an assimilation of Slavic peoples during the period of German expansion eastward during the Middle Ages. Today Germany has become even more ethnically varied by the growth of immigrant communities. Turkish and Yugoslavian groups make up the largest number of immigrants to West Germany in recent years.

Luther and the Reformation

Germany in the Middle Ages

Germany lacked a strong, unifying government in the thirteenth and fourteenth centuries. It was a feudal country, divided into over 300 separate self-governing cities and states ruled by princes, dukes, counts, and bishops. The disputes between these separate rulers were settled by battles, often with troops of German and foreign mercenary soldiers or "robber knights."

While the countryside was in this confusion and chaos, increasing trade brought new prosperity and the growth of a merchant class to the towns. These self-governing towns formed trade associations in which they joined together to encourage trade and protect themselves from plunder and invasion. The most powerful town league was the Hanseatic League, centered in Lübeck and northern coastal towns like Hamburg and Bremen.

The Reformation

A rise in prosperity, coupled with the invention of printing in the mid-fifteenth century, brought the spread of education and literacy throughout Europe. Increasing scientific knowledge and new philosophies began to challenge the authority that religion had held during the Middle Ages. Gradually the era of intense intellectual and artistic activity known as the Renaissance or "rebirth" of art and knowledge began to spread across Europe.

The Catholic Church remained the strongest single force in Germany. Local bishops had the power of lords in some German lands, while the Church, which was controlled from its center in Rome, was wealthy and politically influential.

One of the means by which the Church raised monies was the selling of indulgences, which granted the buyer pardon for a particular sin. The selling of indulgences was the issue that aroused the protest of Martin Luther, the man who was to become the center of the great religious revolution which became known as the Protestant Reformation.

Although Luther himself was excommunicated, the movement for Church reform spread as more people became Protestants. The appeal of Luther's

ideas lay partly in the growing desire of many people to be free of the control, not only of the feudal lords, but also of the Church.

Luther's translation of the Bible into German from Latin was published in 1534. It had a great popularizing effect on the Protestant movement in Germany, and the language Luther used in the translation helped set a standard in the development of modern German.

The Thirty Years' War

By 1618 about half of the German states were Protestant, mostly in northern and eastern Germany. Many individual princes had become Protestant, while the Emperor remained allied with the Church in Rome.

In 1618, a group of Protestants from Bohemia rebelled against the Emperor's rule. An army was raised by Count Wallenstein and General Tilly to crush the rebellion. This was the beginning of the Thirty Years' War (1618–1648), which grew to involve Denmark, Sweden, France, and the Netherlands. What began as a religious war became a series of wars for domination over Europe.

▲ Martin Luther (1483–1546), a priest and professor of theology at the University of Wittenberg, intended at first only to prompt certain reforms within the Church. He began preaching the doctrine of salvation by faith, rather than by good works (that is, giving money to the Church) alone. Luther wrote a paper containing 95 theses or arguments which criticized the Church practice of selling indulgences. He nailed it on the church door in Wittenberg on All Saints' Day 1517, a direct challenge to Church authority. It set off a chain of events which eventually led to his excommunication. Luther went on to question the supremacy of the Pope, and to stress the doctrine of Christianity in which the believer's direct communion with God was valued over the priest serving as an intermediary. Although Luther's ideas spread through Germany quickly, this caricature (left) showing the Devil using Luther to play a tune shows that his ideas also aroused great opposition.

Germany was a battleground for the war and suffered greatly from years of slaughter, plunder, and the plague. When peace came with the Treaty of Westphalia in 1648 two-thirds of its population had been lost, and many villages had completely disappeared. The treaty reaffirmed the sovereigns' rights to determine the religion of their state. The war made Germany even more fragmented than before—there were now over 1800 German states.

▼ While the new middle classes in the towns prospered, the peasants became poorer. As the towns grew, trade increased and money as a form of wealth became more important. The noblemen, whose wealth had been land, wanted more money. Those who were landlords began demanding higher taxes that the peasants could not pay. In 1524 the peasants rebelled against these conditions, against serfdom, and their feudal lords. The revolt began in the Black Forest and spread in a series of uprisings through southern Germany and on to Hesse. Thuringia, and Franconia. The peasants had been encouraged by the teachings of Luther, who preached the "liberty of Christian men," in other words the equality of all men under God. But Luther denounced their revolt when violence turned on the churches and monasteries. Without strong organization the Peasants' Revolt was doomed to failure, and local lords often put down the uprisings with great brutality. The peasants were left worse off at the end of the revolt than they had been at the beginning. Their condition did not improve significantly until the middle of the nineteenth century.

Frederick the Great and Prussia

The rise of Prussia

The most important German state to emerge after the Thirty Years' War was Brandenburg, ruled by the Hohenzollern family. This dynasty encouraged industry and agriculture in their kingdom and raised a large, efficient army. When Brandenburg was joined with the Duchy of Prussia in 1701, its Hohenzollern leader renamed the state the "Kingdom of Prussia."

It was during the lifetime of King Frederick II, or "Frederick the Great," that Prussia emerged as a powerful state and a rival to Austria. Frederick's father had increased Prussia's military power, as well as making the state wealthy. Frederick continued this military tradition during his own reign, as well as succeeding in expanding Prussian territory.

The only state in the old German Empire to rival Prussia was Austria. Frederick saw his chance to challenge Austria's power when the Austrian Emperor died in 1740, leaving his daughter Maria Theresa on the throne. The succession of a female heir was liable to be disputed, a fact Frederick realized when he seized the Austrian province of Silesia in 1740.

Frederick fought against Austria in the War of Austrian Succession (1740–1748), and against Austria, France, and Russia in the Seven Years' War (1756–1763) in order to secure his claim to Silesia. He consolidated the gains of his Prussian Empire when he joined Russia and Austria in the Partition of Poland in 1772. This gave him more territory, making Prussia even larger. When Frederick died in 1786 he had succeeded in making Prussia a major European power.

Napoleon and Prussia

Following the French Revolution of 1789, Prussia and Austria were forced to become allies against Napoleon, who had crowned himself Emperor of France in 1804 and set out to conquer Europe.

Austria and Prussia were defeated at first in the Napoleonic Wars of 1805–1813. Franz II of Austria was forced to abdicate as German Emperor.

This ended the "Holy Roman Empire of the German Nation," which had existed since 1486, but had governed Germany (and Austria) in name only.

Feelings of patriotism and a desire for an independent German nation grew in Prussia and throughout Germany during the Napoleonic Wars, when the French army occupied much of Germany. Napoleon was finally ousted from Prussia at the "Battle of the Nations" at Leipzig in 1813. Prussia was allied with England and Russia against Napoleon; the Prussian army under General Blucher fought alongside the English army under Wellington to defeat Napoleon at the Battle of Waterloo.

The German Confederation

After the Napoleonic wars the German Empire was not restored. Instead a confederation of the German states was established, to be governed by a parliament in Frankfurt.

Hopes that the German Confederation would provide the basis for a united German nation were unfulfilled, for the Confederation still left too much power in the hands of individual princes. The Austrian Chancellor Metternich ensured that opposition to the new Confederation was suppressed and it served as a substitute for a central government for the next 50 years.

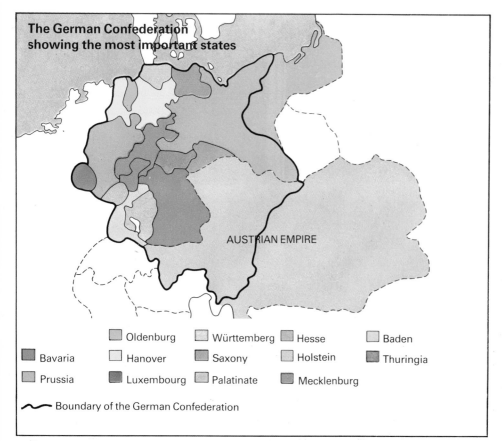

The German Confederation showing the most important states

AUSTRIAN EMPIRE

Bavaria
Prussia

Oldenburg
Hanover
Luxembourg

Württemberg
Saxony
Palatinate

Hesse
Holstein
Mecklenburg

Baden
Thuringia

Boundary of the German Confederation

▲ Germany, after the Congress of Vienna of 1815, which ended the Napoleonic Wars. The German Confederation was a federal union of independent states, consisting of 35 German states and four self-governing cities, ruled by Austria.

◄ Frederick II or "Frederick the Great" (1740–1786) was the leader who brought Prussia to a position of prominence. He was known as an "enlightened despot," for although he was absolute ruler of Prussia, he allowed his subjects certain rights and freedoms. The "Prussian Code of State Law" initiated during his reign abolished serfdom and allowed freedom of religion. It also allowed Jews to own land if they converted to Christianity. Frederick's character was full of contradictions. As a young man he clashed with his strict father, and tried to run away from military training. He was caught by his father's guards and put in an army prison, while his best friend and accomplice was executed. This experience may have shaped Frederick's character— in later life he was embittered and lonely.

► The Battle of Lowositz, October 1756, during the Seven Years' War. The battle, begun in fog, caused heavy losses but the Prussian infantry finally triumphed.

▼ Jena University at the time of Frederick. Education was organized under the government for the first time during his reign.

▲ Frederick was an enthusiastic patron of the arts and surrounded himself with writers and musicians at his palace in Berlin, Sans Souci. The composer Johann Sebastian Bach (1685–1750) was a frequent visitor at Sans Souci, where his son C.P.E. Bach worked as court composer. Frederick himself played the flute, and several concertos were dedicated to him as a flute virtuoso.

◄ The French philosopher Voltaire (1694–1778) with Frederick at Sans Souci. Frederick was an admirer of the French language and scorned the German language, which he spoke poorly. He was a follower of the Enlightenment, the movement that stressed reason and humanitariansim. Frederick said that "philosophers should be the guides of princes," but later he quarreled with Voltaire, arrested him, and tried to confiscate one of his manuscripts.

Bismarck and the unification of Germany

The National Assembly of 1848

News of the French Revolution of 1848 was greeted with wild enthusiasm in Germany. The demand for national unity under a central, democratic government spread.

In March 1848 an assembly of national representatives met in Frankfurt to draft a constitution. The purpose of the National Assembly was to form a new German Republic, but it was unsuccessful and Germany remained divided.

Bismarck and the new German Empire

In 1861 Wilhelm I became King of Prussia. When the parliament objected to his plans to strengthen the Prussian army, he called in Otto von Bismarck to head his ministry. Bismarck carried out the King's plan and became the strength behind the throne, Germany's real leader.

As Prime Minister of Prussia, Bismarck often ignored the wishes of parliament. He had taken part in the Assembly of 1848 and said that it had taught him how useless democratic methods were.

Bismarck created a new German Empire by gaining territory, eliminating Austria as a competitor, and challenging the dominance of France in Europe. The northern territories of Schleswig and Holstein were won from Denmark in 1864. Prussia defeated Austria in the war of 1866, and Austria was expelled from the German Confederation.

Bismarck then set the stage for a unified Germany with the North German Confederation of 1867, which joined 21 German states under Prussia. The growing influence of Prussia threatened France, which declared war. When the states of southern Germany joined Prussia and the northern states in the Franco-Prussian War of 1870, all of Germany was united against a common enemy. The new "German Empire" was declared after the defeat of France in 1871. Wilhelm I became Emperor (*Kaiser*) and Bismarck was made Chancellor.

Wilhelm II succeeded his father as *Kaiser* in 1888. The young *Kaiser* was ambitious but politically inexperienced. His actions led to conflict with Bismarck, who resigned as Chancellor in 1890.

At the turn of the century Europe was a "powder keg" of conflicting interests over industrial growth and the acquisition of territory. Russia, France, and England formed an alliance, an event Bismarck had always tried to prevent. Germany was surrounded by hostile powers, and the world waited in expectation for the spark that would set off another European war.

▲ Proclamation of Wilhelm I as the first Emperor of Germany, 1871, in the Hall of Mirrors at Versailles.

▼ An illustration showing German forces in Africa, 1891. Wilhelm II wanted to acquire foreign colonies, but Germany came late to the European competition for African territories.

▲ Otto von Bismarck (1815–1898), a master strategist. Wilhelm II continued Bismarck's foreign policy, but succeeded only in surrounding Germany with hostile powers, setting the stage for World War I.

▼ When the Austrian archduke Franz Ferdinand was shot by a Serbian nationalist in 1914, Austria declared war on Serbia. Russia and France came to Serbia's defense, and Germany joined on the side of Austria. When Britain entered the war against Germany, it was thought that the war would be over in six weeks. Instead it went on for four years, and was one of the most devastating wars the world had yet known. Soldiers battled from the trenches, facing barbed wire, machine guns, and shrapnel.

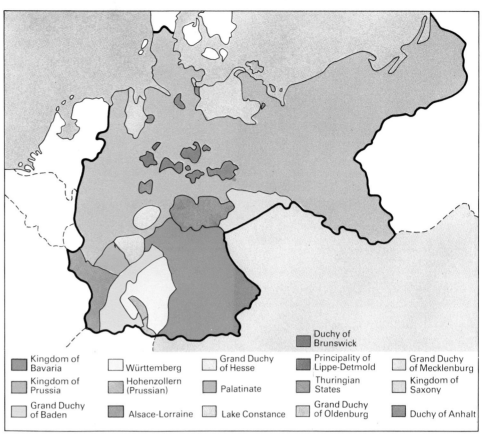

Kingdom of Bavaria	Württemberg	Grand Duchy of Hesse	Duchy of Brunswick
Kingdom of Prussia	Hohenzollern (Prussian)	Palatinate	Principality of Lippe-Detmold
Grand Duchy of Baden	Alsace-Lorraine	Lake Constance	Thuringian States

Grand Duchy of Mecklenburg

Kingdom of Saxony

Grand Duchy of Oldenburg

Duchy of Anhalt

▲ The new German Empire in 1871, after the territorial gains of the Franco-Prussian War. Twenty-one northern German states were joined under Prussia in the North German Confederation of 1867. Alsace and Lorraine were annexed from France.

▼ The siege of Mont Valerien, in Paris, January 1871. After the defeat of the French at Sedan, the German army closed in on Paris. The war ended with the surrender of these forts, and a peace treaty agreed at Versailles.

Hitler and the Third Reich

The Weimar Repubic

The Treaty of Versailles of 1918 imposed harsh settlements on Germany for its part in World War I. Territory was lost, the size of the military was drastically reduced, and Allied troops occupied a corridor on both sides of the Rhine. Germany was obliged to make huge war reparation payments to the Allies. These conditions embittered many Germans.

The government of the new German Republic was formed under the leadership of Social Democrat Friedrich Ebert. A constitution that had been drafted in the town of Weimar was adopted. Various groups, from the communists to right-wing factions of the army, attempted to overthrow the government. Every political party in the country—there were between 30 and 40—was represented in parliament, and the resulting coalition government made agreement on almost any issue impossible.

The Weimar government printed huge amounts of paper money to meet the demands of the war debt. Inflation soared, and the economy was ruined. Before the war the exchange rate for one American dollar was 4.20 marks. By 1923 one dollar was worth over 4200 million German marks.

Rise of the Nazis

The National Socialist German Workers' Party, or Nazi party, rose to power from small beginnings. It began in 1920 in Munich with just a few members under the leadership of Adolf Hitler, an ex-army corporal who had served in World War I. Hitler built up the party, adopting the *Swastika* as its symbol, and recruiting the S.A. or Storm Troops as a private army.

The Nazis failed the first time they tried to take power in the "Beer Hall Putsch" of November 9, 1923 in which 600 Nazis attempted to take over the government of Bavaria. The Nazi leaders were arrested, but Hitler served only nine months in prison, where he wrote his book *Mein Kampf* (My Struggle). In his book Hitler said that the next

time, the Nazis would use democratic means to overthrow the government.

The mass unemployment caused by the Great Depression of the 1930s gave Hitler the chance he was waiting for. Because the Nazis had never been part of the coalition government of the Weimar Republic, they could blame all the other political parties for Germany's problems. By 1932 the Nazis had emerged as the strongest party in Germany, and held 230 seats out of 608 in the Reichstag or Parliament. Hitler became Chancellor under President von Hindenburg and once in office consolidated his power by arresting or murdering his political opponents. Without consulting the Reichstag he made laws that were designed to keep the Nazis in power. Hindenburg died in 1934 and Hitler declared himself *Führer*, leader of Germany. He set out to rebuild Germany, and to take over Europe to create a new German Empire.

World War II

In 1938, after Hitler had established an alliance with the Italian dictator Benito Mussolini, he proceeded with plans to take over Austria. It was Hitler's argument that the new German nation needed more *Lebensraum* (living space), and that he also had the right to annex parts of Czechoslovakia because of the German population living there.

Britain and France wanted desperately to avoid war and tried to negotiate with Hitler over the invasion. Finally, when the German army invaded Poland on September 1, 1939, these two countries declared war on Germany. The United States joined the Allies in 1941, and eventually the whole world was involved in the war. In 1945 Germany was finally forced to surrender.

ADOLF HITLER

▲ Adolf Hitler (1889–1945), one of the single most influential figures in world history, saw himself as a great man destined to lead a great nation. He said that in war anything was justified, and that strong nations had the right to conquer weak ones. Hitler was a brilliant speaker, and well aware of methods for gaining popularity. He used the desire of the "little man" to feel part of a great mass movement, and had no qualms about using propaganda. At the height of his popularity he was revered in Germany as a national hero.

▼ German troops invade Austria, March 1938. The Austrian government tried to prevent the take-over, but was too weak to withstand Nazi pressure from inside the country. This photograph shows German troops being welcomed by Austrian supporters of the Nazi party.

▲ Anti-semitism, or racial prejudice against Jews, had existed not only in Germany, but throughout Europe for centuries before the Nazis. Jews first settled in Europe during the early Middle Ages and by the nineteenth century many Jews were assimilated into German culture. Jewish people participated in every profession, and intermarriage between Jews and Gentiles, or non-Jews, was common.

Nevertheless, Hitler found it easy to use anti-semitism to achieve his own ends. In his speeches he blamed the Jews for all of Germany's problems. His propaganda minister issued vicious attacks on the Jews, and Hitler promoted the myth of the blonde-haired Aryan super-race.

Anti-Jewish laws were enacted when the Nazis came to power. Jews were forbidden to mix with non-Jews. In 1933 shops and businesses owned by Jews were labeled "For Jews Only." Jews were required to wear a yellow star identifying themselves as Jews. Persecution grew much worse after *Reichskristallnacht*, or "Night of the Broken Glass," of November 10, 1938, during which the Nazis organized the looting and burning of Jewish homes, shops, and synagogues.

Concentration camps were built and Jews were sent there to do "forced labor." Instead, they were murdered in mass numbers. Most of the concentration camps, like Auschwitz in Poland, were established in Eastern Europe. As soon as the Nazis invaded a country they began rounding up the Jews, who were joined in the camps by other racial minorities like the Gypsies, as well as people who worked against the Nazi regime, such as Christian pacifists and communists. About six million Jews died in the camps, the results of the most formally organized act of genocide yet known in world history.

▲ Hitler signed a non-aggression pact with the Soviet leader Josef Stalin in 1939. None the less he later broke it by invading the Soviet Union in the summer of 1941. The Russian winter hindered the German army. They were defeated at Stalingrad at the cost of hundreds of thousands of Russian and German troops.

▲ Defeated Germany in June 1945. Allied bombing had destroyed housing, roads, railways, and factories. Food, gasoline, and coal were scarce. In towns and cities women worked in teams to clear away the rubble with their bare hands. People were forced to aid the garbage trucks looking for refuse they could put to practical use.

▶ The post-war partition of Germany. The Soviet Union had advanced into Germany from the east and the other Allies from the west. The Soviet and western Allied areas of occupation became two separate countries in 1949 after disagreements on what form of government there should be in Germany after the war.

Germany after World War II

Hamburg

Berlin

EAST GERMANY

Bonn

WEST GERMANY

West Germany today

The division of Germany

When World War II ended, Germany was divided into four zones of occupation by the invading Allied powers: Britain, France, the United States, and the Soviet Union. The Allies took over the administration of Germany with the objective of preventing the country from ever being able to wage another war.

According to the agreements made by the Allies at the Potsdam Conference of July/August 1945 before the end of the war, the divisions of occupation were for administrative purposes only. However, when agreements broke down between the Soviet Union and the other allies, the division between the Soviet zone in the east and the three western zones of occupation became permanent.

Formation of the Federal Republic

The British and American zones were united for economic purposes in 1947; the French zone merged with them in 1949. Out of this the future state of West Germany was to grow.

A temporary constitution, or "Basic Law" for the new government of West Germany was drawn up by a coalition of representatives from the various states (Länder) in the western zones. The Basic Law, which has much in common with the constitution of the United States, was designed to allow the Länder wide powers, while reserving some important matters for the federal government.

The Basic Law stated that it was to be a temporary constitution until a government uniting both Germanies could be formed. The Federal Republic was declared on May 23, 1949. Elections were held for a federal Bundestag or parliament, and the new federal government was centered in Bonn. Konrad Adenauer became the first chancellor of the Federal Republic, and its first president was Theodor Heuss.

The Federal Government was granted sovereignty from the authority of the Western Allies in 1955. The former four occupying powers have retained the right to decide on the future of Berlin and the possible reunification of Germany.

West Germany today

World War II had a devastating effect on the country. Things had to change quickly after the war. About 40 percent of the housing had been destroyed, and a generation of people had been killed or uprooted by the war. The values and concerns of today's Germans are very different from those of the pre-1945 generation.

One of the issues that worries Germans today is the nuclear arms race. The West German government has close relations with the United States. Sandwiched between East Germany and the Soviet Union on one side and its involvement with the United States and NATO on the other, West Germany is in the middle of the cold war and the arms race.

Although it has the social problems of drug abuse, unemployment, and conflicts between the German and immigrant population, West Germany is at the same time a noticeably well-ordered society. Visitors to West Germany are pleased to notice that streets are clean, trains are on time, and that things run more smoothly than in many other countries.

West Germany also has what is regarded as one of the best social welfare systems in western Europe. Health insurance is mandatory for people on low incomes, and every family with children receives a "child allowance"—measures that help ensure that the citizens of West Germany live comfortably.

▲ The Greens, a new political party, first won seats in the *Bundestag* in 1983, with an anti-nuclear, anti-NATO, and environmentalist platform. The other parties are the CDU (Christian Democratic Union), CSU (Christian Social Union), SPD (Social Democratic Party), and the FDP (Free Democratic Party).

▼ The '60s and '70s saw a period of left-wing social protest among the German people which began with student protests at the universities. The most startling aspect of the movement was the actions of terrorist groups like the Baader-Meinhof gang. More peaceful forms of protest continue today.

▲ An American army tank in a German village. The FRG became a member of NATO, the North Atlantic Treaty Organization, in 1955. West Germany has a compulsory fifteen-month period of army service for nineteen-year-old males—and American, French, and British troops are still stationed in the country.

◀ The *Bundestag* (West German parliament) in session. The Federal Republic has one central government that unites its self-governing states. Voters elect both the representatives of the state parliaments and representatives to the *Bundestag* in Bonn. In elections for the *Bundestag*, voters have two votes—one for the candidate and one for a political party. Delegates from the *Bundestag* and the state parliaments make up a Federal Convention which meets to elect the President and Chancellor. The President represents the FRG abroad, but the Chancellor is the country's real leader.

Arts, past and present

Music

A remarkably large number of the world's composers have been German. Among the list of famous names are Bach, Mozart, Telemann, Mendelssohn, Schumann, Beethoven, and Brahms.

The age of famous German composers began with the Baroque era. Johann Sebastian Bach (1685–1750) wrote a great deal of music for the organ, mostly music to be performed in church. Contemporaries of Bach were Georg Philipp Telemann, who, it was said, could "write music as easily as some people could write a letter," and George Frideric Handel, who began his career in Germany, but later moved to London.

Talented though they were, at this period in history composers were dependent on wealthy, aristocratic patrons for support, and were often treated little better than servants. J. S. Bach, for example, was placed under arrest because his employer, the Duke of Weimar, did not want him to seek a better position at another court. Composers had to travel frequently, and settle wherever they were offered a good position. Despite public acclaim, many struggled against poverty, ill-health, and unhappiness.

The life story of Ludwig van Beethoven, who is probably the best-known German composer, is an example of accomplishment despite these sorts of difficulties. Born in Bonn in 1770, Beethoven had little formal education. By the age of 19 he was solely responsible for his family's welfare, and supported them with odd jobs as a musician and teacher. Influenced by the example of Mozart, whose music he adored, Beethoven moved to Vienna at the age of 22, where he gained success and recognition.

Gradually, he became completely deaf. Of course this was a particularly difficult hardship for a musician. He was known as a quick-tempered but loyal person. His strong will enabled him to overcome this disability and continue composing. Among his works, the Ninth Symphony remains a well-loved creation of his musical genius.

Literature

The greatest figure to emerge from the rich tradition of German literature is Wolfgang von Goethe (1749–1832). He was influenced by the *Sturm und Drang* (Storm and Stress) movement which emphasized creative freedom and the genius of the individual. This influence can be seen in Goethe's early novel about the romantic suffering of *Young Werther*, which caused a sensation throughout Europe. Some young men even followed the main character's example by committing suicide, and the book was blacklisted by the Roman Catholic Church for many years. Goethe was not only a writer but also an artist and scientist and worked as an administrator for the Duke of Weimar for many years. His master-work is *Faust*, the dramatic poem that took him 60 years to finish.

Goethe's close friend, dramatist Friedrich von Schiller, is also considered a great German writer, as are Heinrich von Kleist and the poet Heinrich Heine. Modern writers include the novelist Thomas Mann (1875–1955), author of *The Magic Mountain*, and Franz Kafka (1883–1924), the German-Jewish writer from Prague, who is best-known for his story *The Metamorphosis*.

Many German writers and artists spent the Hitler years in exile. Among the writers who emerged after the war are the novelists Günter Grass and Heinrich Böll, both known for social commentary and satire.

◀ *The Knight, Death, and the Devil*, an engraving by Albrecht Dürer. Dürer, born in Nuremberg in 1474, was one of Germany's greatest Renaissance artists. He made unique technical innovations in the art of print-making, and produced work that was celebrated both for its elaborate beauty and its attention to detail.

▶ A scene from *Nosferatu* by director Werner Herzog, a film version of the vampire story. Herzog was born in 1942 and is one of the group of the ''New German Cinema'' film-makers who revitalized the post-war German film industry after it collapsed in the 1960's.

▲ *Mother Courage,* a play by Bertolt Brecht, follows the life of a peasant woman during the Thirty Years' War. Brecht's writing was concerned with the fates of ordinary people and strongly influenced by his Marxist beliefs. Opposed to the Nazi regime, he left Germany and spent the 1930s and '40s in exile in California, returning in 1947 to work in East Berlin where he died in 1956.

▶ A painting by Ernst Ludwig Kirchner (1880–1938). Kirchner was one of the leading painters of the new style of painting called Expressionism which began in the 1900's. The Expressionists portrayed human feelings rather than painting the world realistically, as it looked to the eye. They were also critical of the growing militarism of Germany under Kaiser Wilhelm II. Kirchner himself was a member of the ''Brücker'' (the Bridge) group, who were known for their use of brilliant colors. In 1937 his paintings were declared ''degenerate'' by the Nazis, and 639 of his works were confiscated.

Characters of fact and fiction

Folklore

Few countries are richer in legend than Germany. Long before they were written down and recorded by the Brothers Grimm, the stories we now know as *Grimms' Fairy Tales* were part of the oral tradition of German folklore. Today the characters of Sleeping Beauty, Hansel and Gretel, and Rapunzel are known to people all over the world. These stories are simple on the surface, but they often contain a deeper meaning or message.

Medieval Germany was mostly covered with dark forests which made travel difficult and dangerous. The wolf in the forest in "Little Red Riding Hood," for example, may have been used to teach children about a real danger.

Besides providing entertainment, folk-tales also attempted to provide explanations for natural phenomena like avalanches, lightning, or disease in the days before people knew the scientific reasons for these events. They were probably told around the fire at night, after a hard day's work. The stories are often full of suspense, violence, and fantasy.

"The Boy Who Went to Learn to Shudder" is one of the most interesting and memorable of the Grimms' tales. In this story a father has two sons, one of whom is clever, while the younger one is so stupid that he doesn't even know the meaning of fear. Longing to learn what it is to shudder with fear, the younger son spends three nights in a haunted castle and kills an assortment of gruesome ghosts and monsters. His reward is three casks of gold and marriage to a princess, proving that perhaps he was not so stupid after all.

Other German folktales are based on real people. The exploits of Till Eulenspiegel, a vagabond and practical joker, were based on a real person who lived in the fourteenth century. A book written about his adventures was very popular, perhaps because it was always rich and important people who were robbed or made to look silly, while the figure of Eulenspiegel is the individual who triumphs over society.

Heroes of myth and legend

The characters of the myths and legends of ancient Germanic tribes were heroes of long, epic sagas. These larger-than-life characters reflected the values of these early German peoples, who were often at war with each other.

The *Hildebrandslied* is the oldest surviving legend, and dates from the eighth century. The story was written down by monks in the eleventh or twelfth century. It would originally have been a poem recited from memory by a minstrel. The tragic story, which probably has some basis in historical fact, is about the heroic warrior Hildebrand, follower and comrade of the King Dietrich von Bern. By a cruel twist of fate, Hildebrand finds himself opposite his own son Hadubrand in battle. Honor demands that the two fight to the death despite their relationship. The end, in which Hildebrand wins, would have been seen by the ancient Germans as the result of divine will.

▲ Jakob and Wilhelm Grimm were nineteenth-century scholars who wanted to study how the language was spoken in different parts of Germany. They asked peasants to tell them stories and collected the folklore in *Grimms' Fairy Tales*.

▼ A scene from *The Rhinegold*, the first of four operas in *The Ring of the Nibelungs* by Richard Wagner (1813–83) based on ancient German myth. Characters include gods, giants, gnomes, and heroic warriors.

◄ Faust signs a blood pact with the devil in a scene from the play by Johann Wolfgang von Goethe. Faust sells his soul to the devil, Mephistopheles, in exchange for knowledge and experience beyond that of ordinary humans. He is later rescued from having to fulfill his end of the bargain. The famous character in Goethe's play is based on a real-life historical person, a Doctor Faust of the fifteenth century who was rumored to have magical powers.

▼ The popular German writer Karl May (1842–1912) wrote fiction that was read avidly by both children and adults. The main characters of his stories were always Germans who had traveled to far-off lands. They were honest and brave as they fought and battled villains and protected the innocent. May's most famous hero was the gunslinger "Old Shatterhand" in the *Winnetou* stories. May's stories are still quite popular in Germany today.

▼ Ever since the *Ring* was first produced at Bayreuth, directors have been reinterpreting its staging. Here the heroes are dressed as astronauts for their descent below the waters of the Rhine.

Great inventions

rorde:qṁ iṕ ṫaum vidębūr. Beati pa
ciṫici:qṁ filij dei vocabūtur. Beati q̄
pſecuṫionē paṫiūtur ꝓpter iuſticiam:
qṁ ipſoꝝ eſt regnū cęloꝝ. Beati eſtis
cū maledixerint vobis·et pſecuṫi vos
fuerint et dixerūt ōne malū adverſū
vos menṫienṫes ꝓpter me. Baudete ꝛ

The invention of printing

The German invention that has been of greatest benefit to the world was the invention of printing. Block printing, in which text and illustration were carved on a block of wood (one block to a page) had been in use since the early fifteenth century. Until this time books were copied by hand, a laborious process which made them rare and expensive.

The method of block printing was an improvement, but each single block had to be hand-carved and the wooden blocks could only be used between 250 and 300 times. It was still too time-consuming a process to allow mass production of books or other printed material.

Around 1440 a goldsmith named Johann Gensfleisch zum Gutenberg at Mainz, known as Johann Gutenberg, began his experiments with the process of printing. He invented the movable type system, in which separate metal pieces for each individual letter could be locked together to form the words of a page, then taken apart to form the next page.

The first book published by Gutenberg's press was the Holy Bible in 1453. The invention of movable type would later be a great factor in the religious reformation following Martin Luther's revolt against the Church. For the first time everyone, not just monks or priests, had access to the Bible and could read it for themselves.

Philosophers

Germany has produced some of the world's greatest philosophers, a list which includes Immanuel Kant, Arthur Schopenhauer, Georg Wilhelm Friedrich Hegel, and Karl Marx.

Most universally influential among them was Karl Marx, whose philosophy analyzes the economic forces at work in society and urges workers to take control of the means of production through revolution. Living in politically-enforced exile in London from 1849, Marx spent 25 years of his life writing his major work *Das Kapital* with the help of his friend Friedrich Engels.

Scientists

Research and discoveries made by German scientists have been far-reaching. Among the earliest was the astronomer Johannes Kepler (1571–1630) who expanded on the work of Copernicus and Galileo with his laws of planetary motion.

Among physicists there are Max Planck (1858–1947), who developed the quantum theory, and Albert Einstein (1879–1955), one of the world's greatest scientists.

Einstein's theory of relativity had made him internationally famous, yet anti-semitism in Nazi Germany forced him to move to the United States in 1933. Ironically for Einstein, who abhorred war, it was his advice that helped the United States develop the atomic bomb during World War II.

▲ An extract from the Bible printed by Johann Gutenberg (1397–1468). Despite his great skill, Gutenberg was not a good businessman, and his printing works were taken over by his former partner.

▲ Important contributions to medicine have been made by German scientists. One was the discovery of X-rays by Konrad Röntgen (1843–1923), shown above in his laboratory where he first discovered X-rays by accident. X-rays enable doctors to see an image of the inner structure of the body, greatly improving their ability to diagnose everything from cancer to broken bones. Another great development was made by Paul Ehrlich (1854–1915), the founder of chemotherapy. Ehrlich's study of how the human immune system (particularly in the blood) reacts to disease was important in the treatment of what were once incurable diseases: typhoid, malaria, diphtheria, and syphilis.

◄ The zeppelin, named after its inventor Count Zeppelin, was the first successful rigid airship. It was made of hot-air balloons inside a fabric-covered frame, and fitted with a motor. The zeppelin made several successful journeys after World War I. On one trip to Lakehurst, N.J. on May 6, 1937 one zeppelin, *The Hindenberg*, exploded and was destroyed. Thirty-five passengers and one member of the ground crew were killed.

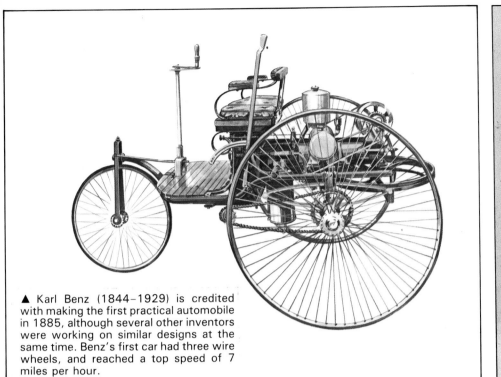

▲ Karl Benz (1844–1929) is credited with making the first practical automobile in 1885, although several other inventors were working on similar designs at the same time. Benz's first car had three wire wheels, and reached a top speed of 7 miles per hour.

▲ A plaque commemorating the house in Trier where Karl Marx (1818–83) was born. Marxism continues to be a deeply influential force in world history and politics.

▼ Walter Gropius (1883–1969) was one of the leaders of the progressive movement in architecture known as "Bauhaus." This 1925 building houses the Bauhaus School of Art and Design in Dessau.

▲ During the seventeenth century the new vogue for drinking tea and coffee added to the demand for porcelain from China. Efforts to manufacture porcelain in Europe were unsuccessful until Ehrnfried von Tschirnhaus, a German nobleman, and his assistant Johann Böttger realized the secret lay in using the right sort of clay. Tschirnhaus opened a factory in Meissen near Dresden in 1708, and soon princes all over Europe had their own porcelain factories.

Industry, technology, and the economy

The economic miracle

Germany was in ruins at the end of World War II. Roads and railway lines had been destroyed by bombing, factories were damaged, and raw materials for industry were scarce. This was what the Germans called "Zero Hour," when they began to rebuild the economy. What they have accomplished since has been called "the economic miracle."

One of the reasons that West Germany was able to rebuild its industry and economy quickly was that it had a large labor force due to the influx of refugees from the East. Another reason was the European Recovery Program, the Marshall Plan, of 1947. This was an American program that gave West Germany, among other countries, financial aid after the war. West Germany received many millions of dollars in aid. West Germans worked hard in the years following the war. The average working week was 48 hours; this was the longest in any western European country. The leadership of the new Federal Republic of Germany, under the Chancellor Konrad Adenauer and Economic Minister Ludwig Erhard, also contributed to economic success. Erhard set up a system that encouraged new investment in West German industry, while Adenauer was active in the formation of the EEC, the European Economic Community, in 1957.

The 1950s and '60s were a period of economic boom for West Germany. Industry was expanding so rapidly that there were soon more job vacancies than people to fill them. The government of the Federal Republic invited guest workers from Italy, Spain, Greece, and Turkey to come to work in West Germany. But technological advances such as computerization and automation reduced the number of jobs available in industry.

Today there is a foreign population of 4.6 million in West Germany. Over 1.5 million of these are Turkish people who have come to West Germany to work, and have settled there. Meanwhile the number of unemployed in West Germany is over a million.

Industry today

The Ruhr River in North Rhine-Westphalia has traditionally been the center of heavy industry in Germany. Its coalfields fed the giant steel-producing factories, like August Thyssen Hutte in Duisburg, the largest producer of steel in Germany before World War II.

Today West Germany's economic strength is no longer dependent upon heavy industry in the Ruhr Valley, but rests upon a variety of industries all over the country. One of West Germany's strengths as a modern industrial nation is a reputation for excellence in design and engineering.

Automobile factories like BMW in Bavaria produce cars that are valued for their quality of design and exported to countries all over the world. New growth industries are in high technology. In the field of electrical engineering, new factories producing sound equipment and electrical appliances have been opened in the southwest around Stuttgart and in Bavaria. The general trend in West German industry today is toward the spread of industry across the country. Computer technology is increasingly important, especially for its uses in industry.

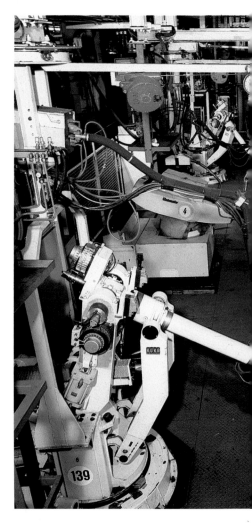

◄ A technician working in the chemical industry. Among the recent developments made in the German chemical industry are the manufacture of new types of plastics and synthetic fibers.

▲ The Hamburg docks: Germany's busiest port and the biggest inland seaport in Europe. Hamburg, situated on the Elbe River, is a center of the shipbuilding industry in West Germany, along with the cities of Bremen and Kiel.

▼ The technological revolution of the post-war period changed agriculture in the FRG, making it both more efficient and prosperous. But in the steep vineyards of the Mosel, grapes must still be picked carefully by hand.

▲ The food industry is one of the FRG's largest. These wine vats at a wine-making company are operated by the latest computer technology.

▲ An automated production line at a Daimler-Benz factory, where robots assemble the car parts. This sort of automation plays an increasingly large part in German industry.

West Berlin

Berlin, the German capital

Berlin grew from small beginnings as a provincial village on the Spree River to become the capital city of Prussia in 1709.

Reminders of its emergence as a Prussian city are the Charlottenburg Palace built by Friedrich I, the magnificent boulevards of Unter den Linden (now in East Berlin), and Kurfürstendamm, built when Berlin became the capital of Bismarck's German Reich of 1871.

Berlin grew very quickly in the nineteenth century, and became a thriving commercial center. At this time it was a city of theaters and opera houses, as well as of miserable slums where people who worked in the factories lived in poverty. A lively nightlife of cafes, cabarets, and nightclubs grew up in Berlin after World War I, when artists and writers were drawn to the city.

Some of the most explosive national events of the 1930's and '40s took place in Berlin. The parliament building, the Reichstag, was burned in 1933, an event the Nazis blamed on their political opponents. Berlin was badly bombed during World War II, and the Berliners showed their toughness in their cheerful humor and determination to survive.

Finally, in April 1945, when defeat for Germany was imminent, Russian troops advanced on Berlin and it is believed that Hitler took his own life in a blazing underground bunker near the center of the city.

The divided city

The end of the war saw hard times for Berlin. Food was scarce, and thousands died from starvation in the months following surrender.

Berlin was the headquarters of the *Kommandantura*, the occupying force of the four victorious Allied nations: the Soviet Union, France, Britain, and the United States. Although it lay inside the Soviet zone of occupation, the city was divided into four zones, each controlled by one of the Allies. The British, French, and American zones were in the west, and the Soviet zone in the east. Arguments over the administration of Germany came to a head in 1948 when the Soviets walked out of negotiations

and blockaded all land routes into Berlin.

The other three countries countered with the Berlin Airlift, a gigantic operation to bring food and supplies to West Berlin, sometimes landing as many as 1,000 planes a day.

East Berlin

West Germany made a rapid economic recovery after World War II, due in large part to millions of dollars in aid from the United States. East Germany lagged far behind, and had to make payments in war reparations to the Soviet Union, which had lost 20 million people in the war against Germany.

Heavy demands were put on the workers in East Germany to increase production and thus improve the economy. In June 1953 workers in East Berlin marched and rioted, protesting against the government's demands. Soviet tanks and troops put down the revolt, but the protest had the effect of improving working conditions.

By 1961, although the border between the two countries was closed, people from East Germany who wished to move to the west could still some-

times manage to escape from East to West Berlin. This was made next to impossible when the Berlin Wall was built by the East German authorities. Today tourists and people from West Berlin may visit East Berlin for a day. People from East Berlin are seldom allowed to visit West Berlin.

West Berlin today

Much of the grand architecture of Berlin was flattened by wartime bombing. During rebuilding it was replaced by tall concrete apartment complexes. A continuing shortage of housing means that more modern buildings are going up all the time.

A fast pace of life and a festive atmosphere ensure that West Berlin is still a vital and exciting city. Its central shopping district, the Kurfürstendamm, has luxurious shops and department stores and outdoor cafes where patrons sit under the trees to drink coffee. Berliners often make a daily ritual of visiting their favorite cafe or pub, for conversation as well as refreshment.

◄ The Berlin Wall is covered with graffiti on the western side. Buildings were razed on the eastern side to create a ''no man's land,'' making escape over the Wall almost impossible. When it was first built in 1961, the Berlin Wall seemed an ominous sign of Soviet aggression to some Western observers. Today, after 25 years of coexistence, Berliners on both sides regard the nine-foot high concrete barrier as a fact of everyday life.

▲ The traditional make-up of West Berlin's population is changing. Young people are attracted to the city's alternative lifestyles, and there is a large community of Turkish guest-workers.

▼ The Kaiser Wilhelm Memorial Church, with its bomb-damaged tower, is a landmark of West Berlin. There is entertainment going on 24 hours a day, so the city is always brightly lit at night.

The Rhine River

The great artery

The Rhine, the most important waterway in Europe, flows through several countries and has a total length of 820 miles. Fed by its tributaries, among them the Main and the Mosel, the Rhine flows through Germany and the Netherlands before entering the North Sea.

The Rhine is a main artery in the canal and waterway systems that connect trade and transportation for all of Europe. This is important to West Germany for it has little shoreline and gains a water-route to the Netherlands and the North Sea via the Rhine.

Self-propelled diesel barges and tugs are the most common vessels on the river. It is not uncommon to see barges that are also family homes, with living quarters in the cabin and washing hung out to dry on deck.

The Rhine and industry

The port at Duisburg on the Ruhr River is the heartland of heavy industry in Germany. It is the largest port on the Rhine-system, and is always filled with freighters and tankers loading and unloading goods for manufacturing.

Coal was once the largest cargo item to be transported. Today oil, ore, building materials, chemicals, and fertilizers are carried up and down the Rhine. Efforts to clean the Rhine's waters have not been effective because factories continue to spill chemicals into the water. It is no longer safe to swim in the Rhine, and the salmon that once thrived there are now gone.

The romantic Rhine

The area between Mainz and Cologne is called the Middle Rhine. There, most of the factories are left behind, and the river flows through beautiful countryside, cutting through hills and passing villages and vineyards.

The Rhineland is famous for producing German wines. The wine festivals and the romantic scenery make this a popular area for tourists.

Along the Middle Rhine there are a number of ruined castles perched on the hilltops overlooking the river. Knights and landlords who owned the land along the river made traders pay tolls, and sometimes sent out raiding parties to rob them. Today some of the castles are used as restaurants, cafes, and youth hostels.

Along some parts of its course, the Rhine becomes quite narrow, and in earlier days hidden rocks and ledges were a danger to boats trying to navigate past these stretches of the river. The German poet Heinrich Heine (1797–1856) drew on one of the old legends about the difficulties of navigation on the Rhine when he wrote the words to the popular folk-song *Die Lorelei*.

Today the river is frequently dredged, and even ocean-going liners of up to 2,000 tons travel the Rhine.

▲ The Lorelei rock where, according to legend, the Lorelei lured boatmen to their death with her singing.

◀ Steamers like this ship, the *Loreley V,* carry passengers up and down the Rhine.

▶ ''Rhineland is wine-land,'' is a German saying that aptly describes this region where so much agricultural land is given over to wine-growing. Over 400,000 gallons of wine are produced in West Germany each year, much of it coming from the Rhineland. Vineyards are a common sight in the Rhine valley and the surrounding wine-growing regions. Vines are planted wherever there is enough sun to ripen the grapes. Once the grapes are harvested in the autumn, they are crushed in mechanical presses. The grape must, or juice, is then allowed to ferment and put into casks, like these shown here, to mature over the winter.

▼ Like many historic buildings in the Rhine valley, the St. Jacobus church in Rüdesheim is surrounded by vineyards.

Home and family

Housing

West Germany, with a population of about 61 million, is one of the world's most populous countries for its size. In terms of living space, this means there is an average of 240 people per square mile.

For people who live in the cities, housing space may be a problem. Many live in newly-built apartment complexes. Although an apartment may not be very spacious, modern German furniture is designed to make the best use of the available space.

A great many houses and apartments were built in Germany in the years following World War II. Many old buildings had been destroyed by bombing. Millions of refugees from East Germany and former German territories in eastern Europe flooded into West Germany, and this rising population added to the housing shortage. Although the shortage officially ended in 1974, housing is still expensive. Those who can afford to may follow the current fashion and have a house custom built.

Family life

A close family life has traditionally been important in Germany. At the same time, people in West Germany are subject to the modern trends in western European societies, such as the rising divorce rate.

One major change in the German family is that it is getting smaller. For every 1,000 people in the FRG, there are only 9.6 births per year. While some families may have 2 or 3 children, many have none at all. The German population is rapidly decreasing, despite government incentives for people to have children, such as long maternity leaves and child allowances.

Religious education is still part of family life and state education in West Germany, although most Germans are not regular church-goers. The numbers of Protestants and Catholics are almost even in West Germany, with more Catholics in the south and more Protestants in the north. A church tax is collected by the state from income tax. People do not have to pay the tax if they are not members of a church, but most are, and choose to pay the tax.

The day of Confirmation, when a young person becomes a member of his or her church, is an important day for both Protestant and Catholic families. Children who have just been confirmed are usually given a party and presents to celebrate the event.

Shopping

West Germans enjoy the highest standard of living in Europe, and in general can afford not only the necessities of life, but also many luxury items. Goods produced in West Germany are usually made to high standards of manufacture and design.

West Germans are usually neatly and fashionably dressed. The latest stylish clothing is available in the large, well-stocked department stores or in small boutiques.

In the early 1960s German streets were lined with small shops like bakers, butchers, dairies, and tobacconists. These shops are gradually being replaced by supermarkets and shopping malls. There are fewer street vendors today than in the past, and the era of the door-to-door merchants is over as well.

Most towns and cities have a busy central shopping area with underground parking and a bustling pedestrian zone.

▲ A German family gathers for the midday meal. In this family, in which there are grown-up children, parents and children work together to bring in the harvest on the wine-estate. It has been in their family for generations.

► A modern housing development. Although the German countryside is beautiful, the high population density means that little of it has remained untouched. Groups of houses or cottages like these are planned to blend with the environment.

◄ A German kitchen, with all modern conveniences. The role of housewife and mother has traditionally been important to German women. However, today women account for 38 percent of the workforce, but half-day school hours mean that mothers with young children may still need to be at home in the afternoon.

► Every German town has its market square, where goods are sold from open stalls on market days. Many people prefer to shop in this way if they can. Plants are very popular in German homes and they are usually available for sale at the flower stalls. It is a polite custom to bring a gift of fresh flowers when visiting friends, especially for Sunday afternoon cake and coffee.

Eating the German Way

Food and health

Nowadays most Germans live in towns or cities and have office or indoor jobs. They are not as physically active as earlier generations were, and so need to eat fewer calories. As a result the modern German diet is becoming lighter and less filling.

Germany suffered from a shortage of food after World War II. Many older people can remember having nothing to eat but potatoes for weeks on end. When West Germany was prosperous again in the 1960s, the desire to make up for earlier hardships led to what was called the "eating wave."

Just like many Americans, West Germans are now very conscious about keeping their weight down for reasons of health and fashion. New diets are always being printed in magazines and the thermal-spring health resorts are always full of people taking mineral water "cures" and going on diets.

National foods

Most cultures have a traditional starch that makes up the bulk of its diet. In Germany these are varied—bread, dumplings, and potatoes. Pork is by far the most popular type of meat eaten in Germany, followed by beef and veal. Dairy products are also important. A variety of good cheeses are available.

Germans are fond of good beer and they drink a lot of it—about 158 quarts per person each year—most of it high-quality beer made by small local breweries. German wines are also popular.

Foreign foods are adding a new variety to the West German diet. Every city now has its Chinese and Turkish restaurants and American-style hamburger stands.

Daily meals

The day begins with a small breakfast of fresh coffee or tea, and a crusty white roll, called *Brötchen*. Traditionally bakers would deliver fresh hot rolls first thing in the morning, but nowadays most people buy fresh bread from the bakery as often as possible.

Most children take a sandwich with them to school to eat at mid-morning as a "second breakfast," and then go home for a hot dinner at midday after school is out. The midday meal of one meat dish accompanied, perhaps, by potatoes, gravy, and a cooked vegetable, is traditionally the largest meal of the day.

Supper is a much lighter meal. It may be just soup and cold meat or sausages on open sandwiches, along with tea or beer for the adults and hot chocolate for the children.

Famous regional dishes

▲ Westphalian ham, a speciality of central Germany. Served with pumpernickel bread, it makes a traditional breakfast.

◄ A bakery window shows just some of the 200 varieties of German breads. Germans eat bread at almost every meal and like bread that is dark, whole-grain, and filling.

► An elegant restaurant interior where the famous German *Gemütlichkeit* or warm hospitality reigns. Dining out is popular and there is always a good restaurant or *Bierstube* (pub) nearby.

▼ A sparkling-clean delicatessen offering a variety of German meats and sausages. There are dozens of varieties of German sausages to choose from: they may be eaten sliced, spread, poached, or fried. They vary from the delicate *Weisswürste* made with veal to *Getrüffelte Gänseleberwurst*, goose-liver sausage flavored with truffles.

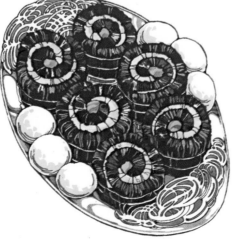

▲ Fish dishes are popular in northern Germany near the sea. These are Rollmops, salted herring fillets, prepared with spices, onions, and pickles, and soaked in brine.

▲ Roulade. This Rhineland dish is made with strips of rump steak filled with bacon, onions, and pickled cucumber. It is often eaten with hot boiled red cabbage and "fluffy" dumplings.

▲ Black Forest cherry cake or *Schwarzwälder Kirschtorte:* layers of chocolate sponge cake filled with black cherry jam and whipped cream, soaked in cherry liqueur, and topped with chocolate.

Schools and education

High Standards

Each of the ten states of the FRG is responsible for its own education system, so curricula may differ from state to state. State schools, which are free, usually have very high standards, and there are few private schools.

The German school system is mainly a selective one, and the sort of secondary education children receive depends upon their performance in primary school. There are, however, comprehensive schools in some states.

There is a shortage of places at the universities, and students taking the *Abitur* examination feel the pressure of competing for one of those places.

The school day

The first day at school is something every German child remembers. Before setting out each child receives a cone made of cardboard and colored paper filled with candies and toys. Then work begins in earnest. Attendance records are strict and lessons are thorough. Tests are marked from 1 to 6, 1 being the highest.

The school day begins at 8 o'clock and ends in the early afternoon when children go home for a hot lunch. There is a mid-morning break for sandwiches, called the "second breakfast." There are often lessons on Saturday mornings as well.

For many parents the school years are an anxious time. They want their children to succeed at school and go on to a university, for university graduates have a high social status and access to better jobs. Grades are very important for getting jobs later on. Applicants are only considered for most jobs if they have had professional training, with good test scores.

The West German school system

Most children begin primary school at age six. At ten they go to *Hauptschule, Realschule,* or *Gymnasium.*

Hauptschule, or secondary school, provides further general education up to age 16. Apprenticeships are combined with coursework up to age 18.

Realschule, or middle school, lasts for six years, preparing students for careers in business and industry.

Aufbauschule provides more advanced technical instruction for some pupils of the *Realschule.*

Gymnasium (grammar or high school) is for students who want to go on to a university. Separate schools specialize in courses in languages, classics, or science. A nine-year course in at least eight different subjects leads to the *Abitur* examination at the age of 18 or 19. Examinations are often followed by a party to celebrate the end of schooldays.

▲ A classroom in a Munich school. After the war many schools had to be rebuilt, and the opportunity was taken to introduce modern equipment. At the same time a great deal of thought was given to the modernization of the educational system. One example of the changes made in West German schools has been in the friendlier and more informal relations between teachers and students. Teacher-training is specialized. Teachers may only teach subjects they have studied at a university, and must pass a two-year trial period when they begin teaching. Compared with many other countries, teachers in the FRG are well-paid and enjoy good benefits and a high professional status.

◀ Although some universities in West Germany are very large (Munich is the largest, with 38,000 students), there is still a shortage of places even for students who have received high scores on their *Abitur.*

◄ A gymnasium in a modern German school. The newly-built schools are much better equipped with facilities for physical training. The arrangement of the school day, which ends very early in the afternoon, makes it difficult to fit physical training and sports into the curriculum. In general, basic subjects like math and German are considered more important in primary schools than physical education, art, and music. Children are first taught to write in longhand, rather than to print. Classes in religious education are offered, but are not compulsory.

▼ Frequent school field trips are an enjoyable part of school life in the FRG. Trips may include a visit to a place of historical interest like the Roman gate in Trier, shown here, or even a visit to a foreign country. Even young children must do homework. They carry their books and lessons to school and back in a satchel or knapsack.

Sports, leisure, and holidays

Sports

West Germans today have a good deal of free time to pursue leisure activities—the work week is now only 36 hours long, compared with the 48-hour week in the 1950s, and everyone has the right to at least three weeks vacation a year.

Germans enjoy participating in sports. Recreational sports in Germany vary from sailing on the northern coast in the summer to winter skiing in the Bavarian mountains. People enjoy getting into the open air, and many outdoor activities are suited for the entire family.

City parks are full of German sun-worshipers at the height of summertime; but a longing for heat, sand, and sea takes about half the population of West Germany on vacations abroad every year. Among the favorite vacation destinations are Mediterranean beaches in Spain, Greece, and France. Vacations and travel within Germany itself are also very popular.

Festivals and holidays

The year is filled with festivals in Germany, many of them with origins in medieval customs or pre-Christian rituals. The most famous of these are *Karneval* (Carnival) and the *Oktoberfest* in Munich, but every area has its own traditional festivals throughout the year.

Traditionally, practicing Catholics are required to observe strict eating habits and church attendance during Lent, which begins 40 days before Easter. The festival of *Karneval*, as it is called in the Rhineland, or *Fasching* as it is called in Bavaria, begins in February just before Lent.

Elaborate planning goes into the celebration of *Karneval*. Committees are formed to organize masked balls, parties, contests, and parades. When the festival finally arrives, people take to the streets in funny costumes. The tradition of *Karneval* gives ordinarily sober citizens a chance to relax and behave in a silly fashion for a few days every year.

Perhaps the most important of the holidays in Germany is Christmas, which is still celebrated in the traditional way. The decorated Christmas tree brightly lit with candles is an ancient custom that originated in Germany and has more recently become a part of Christmas in many other countries.

▲ There are many green public parks in Germany. Those that are on the grounds of old castles or historic parks are called open-air museums. Germans are nature-lovers who enjoy walking or hiking in the open air. Nature parks with footpaths are very popular, and on Sundays entire families drive out of the city for a walk in the woods or countryside. Summertime is especially pleasant in the public parks, when free concerts and festivals are held outdoors.

◀ The start of an amateur cycling race in Biberach. Cycling is a popular sport in West Germany, and has always been a form of transportation as well. Many public roads have a special lane at the side for cyclists and people on mopeds.

▲ Clubs play a large part in recreational activities for both young and old. Men may belong to a *Schützenverein*, or rifle club, which will hold competitions or sponsor festivals and traveling fairs like the one above. Teenagers may belong to a youth club, perhaps sponsored by one of the churches, where they go to meet and talk, listen to music, or have a bite to eat.

◀ Soccer is the most popular spectator sport in Germany, and fans follow their teams with enthusiasm. Many people also play soccer for recreation. Almost a quarter of the population belongs to some kind of a sports club, and among these, soccer clubs have the most members.

Reference

FACTS AND FIGURES

Land and people

Full title: Bundesrepublik Deutschland (Federal Republic of Germany).

Position: Between 6° and 14° E and 47°, 30° and 55° N. Occupying central position between Denmark and Switzerland and between France and Eastern Europe. West Germany has frontiers with nine other countries.

Flag: Black, red, gold (horizontal stripes).

Anthem: *Einigkeit, und Recht, und Freiheit* (words by H. Hoffmann, 1841; tune by Haydn, 1797).

Constituent parts: The Republic, comprising ten states (*Länder*) and West Berlin (a *Land* of the Republic, but not yet formally incorporated).

Area: 95,982 sq miles, of which West Berlin is 185 sq miles.

Population: 61.4 million of which West Berlin has two million.

Capital: Bonn (pop. 283,891).

Language: German.

Religion: Almost equally divided between Protestants (49 percent) and Catholics (44.6 percent). 0.005 percent are Jewish.

The state: The Basic Law of the Federal Republic was signed on May 23, 1949. It created a republican democratic state, based on the rule of law. It is provisional in that, if Germany is ever reunified, the entire German people would have to approve it.

Political system: Parliamentary democracy, based on a system of direct universal elections, and guaranteed by the Basic Law of the constitution.

Armed forces: Total 490,000: army 341,400, including territorial army; navy 38,050; air force 110,550. About half of the strength of the armed forces is made up of men liable for basic service of 15 months. The United States, France, and the United Kingdom maintain defense forces at bases in West Germany.

International organizations: West Germany became a member of the United Nations in September 1973. Also member of the European Economic Community (EEC), North Atlantic Treaty Organization (NATO), and the Organization for Economic Cooperation and Development (OECD).

The climate of West Germany

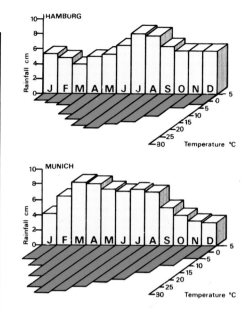

Much of West Germany has a climate not unlike the Northeastern U.S., although winters are colder. The highest peaks of the Alps and the southern German highlands are snow-covered from January to March; the highest summer temperatures are reached in the sheltered lowlands. The mean temperature throughout the year is about 48°F.

Industry in West Germany

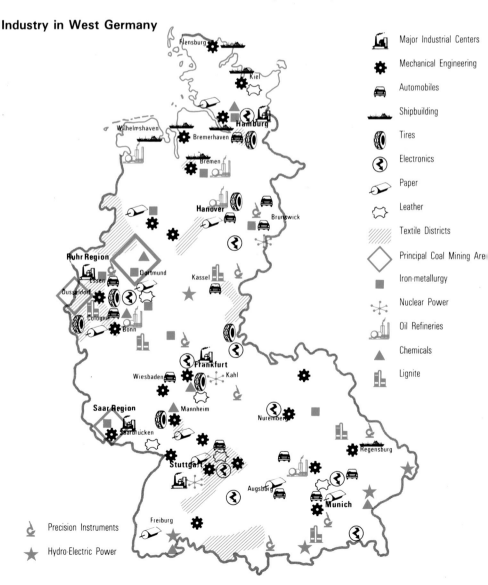

Index

Numbers in **heavy** type refer to captions and illustrations.

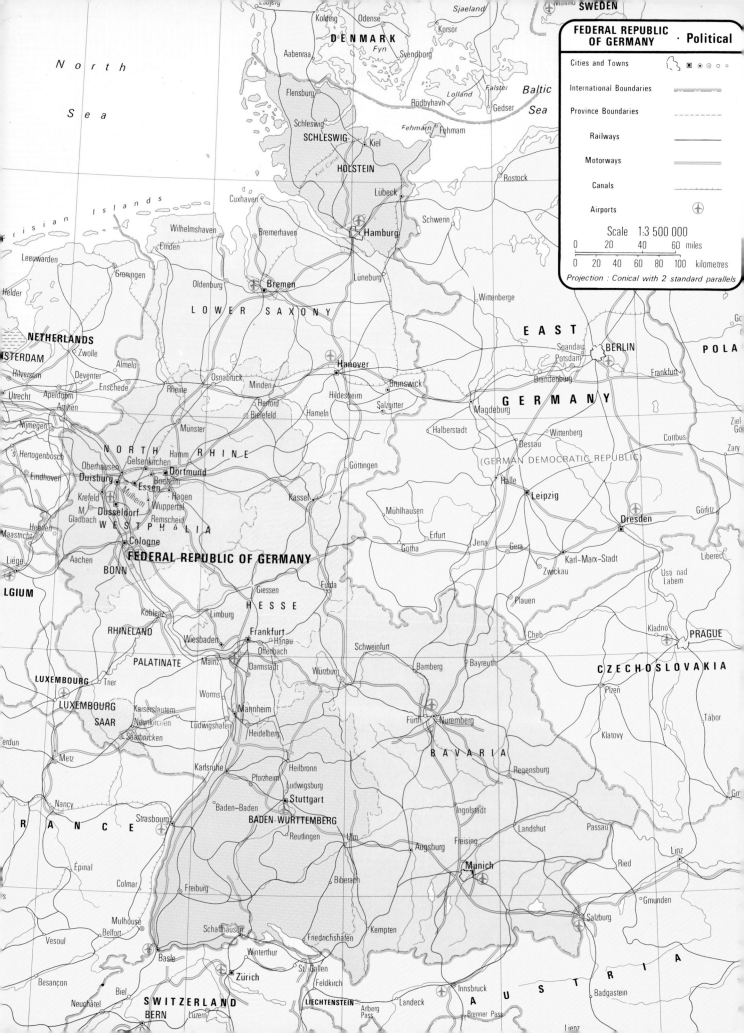

North
Sea

risian Islands

DENMARK

Esbjerg
Kolding
Odense
Korsør
Svendborg

Aabenraa
Fyn

Flensburg
Lolland
Rødbyhavn
Falster
Gedser

Schleswig
Fehmarn Fehmarn

SCHLESWIG-
Kiel

HOLSTEIN
Lübeck
Schwerin

Cuxhaven
Bremerhaven
Hamburg

Wilhelmshaven
Emden

Leeuwarden
Groningen

Oldenburg
Bremen
Lüneburg

LOWER SAXONY

Wittenberge

NETHERLANDS
Zwolle
Almelo
Osnabruck
Minden
Hanover
Brunswick
Hildesheim
Salzgitter

Hilversum
Deventer
Enschede
Rheine

Utrecht
Apeldoorn
Arnhem
Nijmegen

's-Hertogenbosch
Eindhoven

Herford
Bielefeld
Hameln
Hamm

Münster
Göttingen
Kassel

NORTH RHINE
Gelsenkirchen
Dortmund
Bochum
Oberhausen
Essen
Duisburg
Mülheim
Hagen
Krefeld
Wuppertal
M
Dusseldorf
Remscheid
Gladbach
WESTPHALIA

Heerlen
Cologne
Maastricht
Aachen

BONN

Liège
LGIUM
RHINELAND
Koblenz
Limburg

Giessen
Fulda

HESSE

Wiesbaden
Frankfurt
Mainz
Offenbach
Darmstadt
Schweinfurt
Würzburg

PALATINATE

LUXEMBOURG
Trier
Worms

LUXEMBOURG
SAAR
Kaiserslautern
Neunkirchen
Mannheim
Ludwigshafen
Saarbrücken
Heidelberg
Bamberg
Bayreuth

erdun
Metz

Karlsruhe
Heilbronn
Pforzheim
Ludwigsburg
Fürth
Nuremberg

FEDERAL REPUBLIC OF GERMANY

BAVARIA

Nancy
Baden-Baden
Stuttgart
BADEN-WÜRTTEMBERG

Strasbourg
Reutlingen
Ulm
Augsburg
Ingolstadt
Landshut
Passau

Épinal
Freising

Colmar
Freiburg
Biberach
Munich

Mulhouse
Belfort
Schaffhausen
Kempten
Salzburg

Vesoul
Fredrichshafen

Besançon
Biel
Basle
Winterthur
St. Gallen
Feldkirch
Innsbruck
Badgastein
Landeck
AUSTRIA

Neuchâtel
SWITZERLAND
Zürich
Luzern
LIECHTENSTEIN
Arlberg Pass
Brenner Pass

BERN

SWEDEN

Baltic Sea

Rostock

EAST
Spandau
BERLIN
Potsdam
Brandenburg

GERMANY
Magdeburg

Halberstadt

(GERMAN DEMOCRATIC REPUBLIC)
Dessau
Wittenberg
Cottbus
Zary

Halle
Leipzig
Görlitz
Liberec

Mühlhausen
Dresden

Erfurt
Gotha
Jena
Gera
Karl-Marx-Stadt
Zwickau
Usti nad Labem

Plauen

Cheb
Kladno
PRAGUE

CZECHOSLOVAKIA
Plzeň

Tábor

Klatovy

Regensburg

Linz
Ried
Gmunden

POLA
Frankfurt

Ziel
G...

Go...

RANCE

Lienz

FEDERAL REPUBLIC OF GERMANY · **Physical**

Cities and Towns

International Boundaries

feet		metres
9000		2743
6000		1829
3000		914
1000		366
500		183
0		0

Mountain Peaks
▲ 4511

Below sea level

Scale 1:3 500 000

0   20   40   60 miles

0 20 40 60 80 100 kilometres

Projection : Conical with 2 standard parallels

North Sea

DENMARK

SWEDEN

Esbjerg
Kolding
Odense
Korsør
Sjaeland
Malmö

Aabenraa
Fyn
Svendborg
Rödbyhavn
Lolland
Falster
Gedser
Baltic Sea

Flensburg
Schleswig
Kiel Bay
Fehmarn
Belt
Fehmarn
Fehmarn

Kiel
Kiel Canal
Lübeck Bay
Rostock

Heligoland
Bay
Cuxhaven
Lübeck
Schwerin

Frisian Islands

Wilhelmshaven
Bremerhaven
Hamburg

Leeuwarden
Emden
Elbe
Lüneburg
L. Müritz

Groningen
Oldenburg
Bremen
Wittenberge

Helder
NETHERLANDS
Zwolle
Almelo
Aller
Weser
EAST
Spandau
Potsdam
BERLIN
POLA

AMSTERDAM
Deventer
Enschede
Rheine
Osnabrück
Hanover
Brunswick
Magdeburg
Brandenburg
GERMANY
Frankfurt
Spree

Hilversum
Apeldoorn
Arnhem
Minden
Hildesheim
Salzgitter
Halberstadt
Wittenberg
Dessau
Zie
G

Utrecht
Waal
Nijmegen
Maas
Münster
Herford
Bielefeld
Hameln
Teutoburger Wald
Göttingen
Brocken
3750
Harz Mts
Halle
Leipzig
Cottbus
Zary

's Hertogenbosch
Hamm
Gelsenkirchen
Dortmund
Bochum
Kassel
Mühlhausen
Erfurt
Jena
Gera
Karl-Marx-Stadt
Dresden
Görlitz

Eindhoven
Oberhausen
Duisburg
Essen
Hagen
Ruhr
Gotha
Zwickau
Erz Gebirge
Usti nad Labem
Liberec

Krefeld
Mülheim
Wuppertal
Remscheid
Rothaar Geb ▲2760
FEDERAL REPUBLIC OF GERMANY
Thuringian Forest
Plauen
Neisse

M. Gladbach
Düsseldorf
Heerlen
Cologne
Westerwald
Lahn
Giessen
Vogels Berg ▲2533
Fulda
▲3115
Rhön
Fichtel Geb
Cheb
Kladno
Labe (Elbe)
PRAGUE

Maastricht
Aachen
BONN
Rhine
Koblenz
Limburg
Taunus
Wiesbaden
Frankfurt
Hanau
Offenbach
Schweinfurt
Bamberg
Bayreuth
3445
CZECHOSLOVAKIA

Liège
BELGIUM
ennes
Eifel
Mosel
Hunsruck
Mainz
Darmstadt
Spessart
Würzburg
Main
J u r a
Fürth
Nuremberg
Plzeň
Tábor

LUXEMBOURG
Trier
Worms
Ludwigshafen
Mannheim
Heidelberg
Bohemian Forest
Klatovy

Verdun
LUXEMBOURG
Kaiserslautern
Neunkirchen
Saarbrücken
Regensburg
▲4780
Vltava
G

Metz
Karlsruhe
Heilbronn
Ludwigsburg
Stuttgart
Danube
Isar
4521

LORRAINE
Nancy
Pforzheim
Baden-Baden
Reutlingen
Ulm
Ingolstadt
Landshut
Passau
Linz

FRANCE
Strasbourg
ALSACE
Black Forest
Swabian Jura
J u r a
Augsburg
Freising
Munich
Ried

Épinal
Colmar
Freiburg
Biberach
Iller
Amper
Gmunden
Enns

Vosges
Mulhouse
Belfort
Schaffhausen
Friedrichshafen
Kempten
Salzburg

Vesoul
Basle
Winterthur
Bodensee
CARINTHIA

Besançon
Doubs
Biel
Aare
Zürich
St. Gallen
Feldkirch
Innsbruck
Glockner
Badgastein
Lienz

Neuchâtel
Luzern
SWITZERLAND
BERN
LIECHTENSTEIN
Landeck
Brenner Pass
TYROL
AUSTRIA

Impreso por:
Edime, Org. Gráfica, S. A.
(Móstoles) MADRID

Depósito Legal: M. 975-1988
I.S.B.N.: 84-599-2226-X (rústica)
I.S.B.N.: 84-599-2227-8 (cartoné)

IMPRESO EN ESPAÑA
PRINTED IN SPAIN